The Christology of The Shepherd of Hermas:
Investigating the Shape of Early Christology

The Christology of *The Shepherd of Hermas*

Investigating the Shape of Early Christology

Mina Fouad Tawfike
BA, BTh, MA, MTh

AGORA
UNIVERSITY
PRESS

The Christology of *The Shepherd of Hermas*: Investigating the Shape of Early Christology

Copyright © 2024 by Agora University Press

All rights reserved. Printed in the United States of America. No part of this book may be used or reproduced in any manner whatsoever without written permission except in the case of brief quotations embodied in critical articles or reviews.

For information contact : aupress@agora.edu
Agora University Press: press.agora.edu

ISBN 978-1-950831-16-6

Printed in the United States of America

HIS HOLINESS POPE TAWADROS II

118th Pope and Patriarch of the great city of Alexandria and the See of St. Mark.

HIS HOLINESS PATRIARCH IGNATIUS APHREM II

Patriarch of Antioch and all the East.

For Fouad, Magda, Maggie, Odet, Chris, Matthew, Emad, Jos Strenghol, and Mary Ghattas

Table of Contents

Abbreviations and Numbering Systems.............8
Chapter One: The Shepherd of Hermas..............12
    Apostolic Fathers...................................12
    Document and Content..........................12
    Reception in the Early Church..................26
    Dating and Place of Origin......................27
    Authorship... 29
      Literary Genre..................................31
    Major Textual Witnesses.........................33
    Textual Transmission.............................35
    Structure...36
    Community & Function..........................37
Chapter Two: Christology 39
    Monotheism..42
    Jesus and Christ...................................43
    The Name and the Son of God..................44
    Angelomorphic and Angelic Christology.....49
    Definitions...50
    Is the Son of God an Angel in the SH.........51
    Son of God and the Holy Spirit.................54

Similitude 5.................................... .58
Spirit Christology in Similitude 5..............60
Non-Christological Reading of
  Similitude 5..65
On the Use of "Spirit"............................69
Conclusion..71
Bibliography...76
About the Author...................................84

Abbreviations and Numbering Systems

Abbreviations in this work follow those of *The SBL Handbook of Style: For Biblical Studies and Related Disciplines*.[1]

    SH   Shepherd of Hermas

    Mand.   Shepherd of Hermas, Mandate(s)

    Sim.   Shepherd of Hermas, Similitude(s)

    Vis.   Shepherd of Hermas, Vision(s)

The SBL Handbook of Style also provides a parallel chart for the two numbering systems of Hermas, the older numbering—which we will use here—and the Whittaker numbering. It is as follows:[2]

---

[1] Billie Jean Collins, *The SBL Handbook of Style: For Biblical Studies and Related Disciplines*, Second (Atlanta, GA: SBL Press, 2014).

[2] Billie Jean Collins, Ibid., 331–32.

Older Numbering	Whittaker Numbering	Older Numbering	Whittaker Numbering
Visions 1.1	1	Mandates 1	26

Older Numbering	Whittaker Numbering	Older Numbering	Whittaker Numbering
1.2	2	2	27
1.3	3	3	28
1.4	4	4.1	29
2.1	5	4.2	30
2.2	6	4.3	31
2.3	7	4.4	32
2.4	8	5.1	33
3.1	9	5.2	34
3.2	10	6.1	35
3.3	11	6.2	36
3.4	12	7	37
3.5	13	8	38
3.6	14	9	39
3.7	15	10.1	40
3.8	16	10.2	41
3.9	17	10.3	42
3.10	18	11	43
3.11	19	12.1	44

3.12	20	12.2	45
3.13	21	12.3	46
4.1	22	12.4	47
4.2	23	12.5	48
4.3	24	12.6	49
5	25		

Older Numbering Similitudes	Whittaker Numbering	Older Numbering	Whittaker Numbering
1	50	9.6	83
2	51	9.7	84
3	52	9.8	85
4	53	9.9	86
5.1	54	9.10	87
5.2	55	9.11	88
5.3	56	9.12	89
5.4	57	9.13	90
5.5	58	9.14	91
5.6	59	9.15	92
5.7	60	9.16	93

6.1	61	9.17	94
6.2	62	9.18	95
6.3	63	9.19	96
6.4	64	9.20	97
6.5	65	9.21	98
7	66	9.22	99

Chapter One

The Shepherd of Hermas

Apostolic Fathers

The term "Apostolic Fathers," as noted by Helmut Koester, is an artificial designation that originated in the Renaissance.³ The first to use it was J. B. Cotelier in AD 1762 in his work *Patres, qui temporibus Apostolids floruerunt.* When this book was republished, its publishers named it *Bibliotheca Patrum Apostolicorum*. This corpus reflects the formation of the earliest Church and its struggles. The books of this corpus are: *Didache, 1 Clement, 2 Clement, Fragments of Papias, Apology of Quadratus, Shepherd of Hermas, Epistles of Ignatius, Epistle of Polycarp, Martyrdom of Polycarp, Epistle of Barnabas,* and *Epistle to Diognetus.*

Document and Content

The Shepherd of Hermas (SH) is one of the earliest Christian apocalypses,⁴ and part of the recent Apostolic Fathers' corpus. The SH contains three major sections: five

---

[3] Paul Foster, *The Writings of the Apostolic Fathers* (Bloomsbury Publishing, 2007), 1.

[4] Apocalyptic literature will be discussed and defined in a subsequent section.

visions, twelve mandates (or commandments), and ten similitudes (or parables).

The book is very important for understanding early Christianity in the second century. It is a rich source for the study of the life of early Christians, canonization, Christology, Trinity, social order, repentance, and other aspects.

Brandon Brinkley's summary[5] of the document will provide us with a full view of the nature and type of the document.

Visions

Hermas records five visions given to him by God and recounts what was revealed to him in each.

1. Hermas begins the story by explaining that he was sold by his father to a woman (Rhode), who, after manumission, he loved as a sister, having but one brief lustful thought in his heart. In a vision, the heavens opened, and the woman appears, telling him that she has been called to accuse him of his wicked thought with which he sinned against her, for even an evil desire is a sin. She tells him to pray for God to heal the sins of him and his household. He then meets an old woman who tells him that, though it is

---

[5] "Shepherd of Hermas Explained | Brandon's Notepad," accessed June 15, 2019, https://brandonsnotepad.wordpress.com/tag/shepherd-of-hermas-explained/.

a sin for the righteous to have evil thoughts, God is far angrier on account of the sins of his household. She then reads to him from a book that contains harsh words for heathens and apostates, and glorifying God, reminding the reader that he has much in store for those who keep his commandments in faith. When she is finished, she is moved to the east in a chair carried by four young men, attended by two others.

2. A year later, Hermas has a second vision of the old woman. He agrees to transcribe her book for the elect, but as soon as he was finished, the book was snatched away from him. After fifteen days of prayer and fasting, the meaning of the writing was revealed to him. His wife and sons have sinned greatly but will repent and be saved when they hear the words revealed to Hermas. Hermas will be saved by his simplicity and self-control, should he remain steadfast. The number of days that the saints may repent is fixed, but not the days that the heathen may be saved. Hermas is to tell Maximus of the coming great tribulation. Those who endure and who do not deny the Lord will be happy; also, the Lord is near those who return to him. A young man then reveals to him that the old woman is the Church (not the Sibyl as he had presumed). Hermas is instructed to write two books.

3. The old woman arranged to meet Hermas in the country in the fifth hour to reveal what he should know. She instructed him to pray for righteousness within his household instead, told her six attendants to go and build, and then told Hermas to sit on her left, the right reserved for those who have already pleased God and are sanctified. She explains that the left is for those who share in the same gifts and promises but who must be cleansed before that may sit with the sanctified.

She then showed him the vision she promised: a host of young men led by her six attendants who were building a mighty tower from square stones. Some were from the depths (the water?) and were perfect; others were from the earth and had defects, and some were altered or even cast away unused. She tries to leave but Hermas presses her to understand. She reveals that the tower is her, the Church. It is built on the water that saves mankind and is supported by the invisible power of the Lord. The young men are the holy angels and the six attendants are the greatest amongst them. The different kinds of stones are the saints and the sinners, ranging from the polished and tight-fitting ones being the clergy who act in unity and the stones castaway being those who are not saved due to their sins. Some stones are found acceptable and others are set aside for a time for various reasons until they become useful for building. The pivotal message in this vision is that repentance and salvation are still possible for those stones cast away, though their repentance must be heartfelt and their ultimate dwelling still outside of the tower. The woman points out seven women: Faith, Self-restraint, Simplicity, Guilelessness, Chastity, Intelligence, and Love. Each is the daughter of the prior. Hermas is chastised for asking if the end had come, for it was clear that he did not understand—the tower had not yet been finished. He is commanded to share the vision given to him.

Hermas yearned to know why the woman appeared very old to him in the first vision and progressively younger in the others that followed. After praying for this to be revealed, and fasting, a young man appeared to him and explained that the age of the woman, that is the Church, was a reflection of his strength in spirit.

4. Another twenty days pass. In this vision, Hermas is confronted by a whale-like beast with fiery locusts in its mouth and four colors upon its head. Hermas places his trust in the Lord and is not harmed. Beyond the beast, he meets the woman. She is now young and dressed in white. She tells him that the beast he saw was a type of tribulation to come. She explains the colors to be four ages of the world: black is the current darkness, red the perishing of the

world by blood and fire, gold is what remains after the test, and white the purity of eternal life.

5. In the last vision, Hermas is visited by an angelic figure dressed like a shepherd. The Shepherd is sent to dwell with him for the remainder of his life and deliver to him the commandments of the Lord.

Mandates

The Shepherd gives the following commandments to Hermas. The numbering of these commandments as twelve is misleading, as they are multifaceted. Commandment Four, for example, spans four chapters, each a paragraph, and covers aspects of both Matrimony and Baptism.

1. Have faith in and fear God. Exercise self-control and put on righteousness.

2. Do not partake in slander. Give to the needy in simplicity.

3. Walk in truth always. Hermas confesses to concealing the truth in the past and is told that since he has now heard the commandment, he must be truthful going forward.

4. Thoughts of adultery and fornication are great sins. It is acceptable to put away (i.e. divorce) an adulterous wife, but to then marry another is adultery. The repentant wife should be taken back, but not frequently. This applies in reverse too—men

and women should be treated the same way. To marry again after the death of a spouse is not a sin, but it is better to remain unmarried. Repentance is wisdom. Some taught that Baptism ("when we descended into the water and received remission of our former sins") was the only time of repentance, but the Shepherd tells Hermas that there is one more opportunity to repent after that.

5. Patience provides a pure place for the Holy Spirit to dwell, aiding in the works of righteousness. In contrast, anger pollutes patience and prepares a home for the devil. Anger does not sway those full of faith but drives the Holy Spirit from those who doubt, leaving such men in a "state of anarchy."

6. Walk the straight path of righteousness. Two angels dwell with every man: one of righteousness and one of iniquity. Trust the former and part ways with the latter.

7. Fear the Lord and not the devil. The one who has power is feared and his work performed by those who fear him.

8. The restraint of evil is righteous, but the restraint of good is a great sin. Examples of good works are listed.

9. Pray over all things and with confidence. Doubt, which is from the devil, is lack of faith. Faith is from God.

10. Grief from doubt "crushes out" the Holy Spirit, but grief that results from the actions arising from anger leads to repentance and salvation. It is best to drive away grief altogether by eliminating both doubt and anger.

11. False prophets ruin the minds of the doubters who become idolaters. True prophets are meek and humble, speaking only when and what God wishes them to speak. False prophets are proud and talkative, speaking when they have something to gain.

12. Cherish good and chaste desires over wicked and evil ones. Avoid covetousness and practice righteousness, virtue, truth, faith, meekness, etc.

The angel tells Hermas to walk in these commandments and to preach them. Hermas questions whether or not men are able to keep these difficult commandments and the angel exposes his doubt.

Parables

1. There is no purpose in gathering possessions beyond necessity in this city (the world), for you will be cast out for not obeying its laws (death). It is better to purchase property (afflicted souls) like that found in your native city (Heaven). Do not covet but do the work of God and be saved.

2. The elm tree (the rich), which does not produce fruit, supports the vine (the poor), which allows it to not just produce fruit (intercessions), but to do so abundantly. In this way, both the rich and the poor do God's work as partners, giving back to God what was given to them, through love.

3. In winter, green trees (living) and withered trees (dead) look alike. This life is winter to the righteous.

4. In summer, the dead trees do not produce fruit or leaves and are burned. The next life is summer to the righteous.

5. A slave (the Son of God) was put in charge of a field (the world) with a vineyard (the people) and was told by his master (the Creator, God the Father) to stake it (place Holy Angels in it to keep the people together) while he was away (until the end of the age). He also weeded (removed sins from) the vineyard to please the master with its beauty. His obedience gained the slave his freedom, but the good he performed prompted the master to make him a co-heir with his own son (the Holy Spirit) as well. The master sent the slave many dishes (the commandments of Christ) from his table, and the slave shared the leftovers with his fellow slaves, which also pleased the master. Fasting in and of itself is not true fasting; instead, true fasting is avoiding sin, serving the Lord, keeping His commandments, walking in His ways, and believing

in Him. Therefore, for a fast to be true, the money saved through this self-sacrifice should be given to someone in want. It is explained that Christ is not in the form of a slave, but of a powerful ruler. To sin is to defile the flesh, and thus, the Holy Spirit that dwells within.

6. In a vision, Hermas is shown, two other shepherds. The first tends to sheep that feed in luxury, some of which skip around merrily. This is "the angel of luxury and deceit" and the skipping sheep represent men who have been deceived and have "freed" themselves from God. The second, savage in appearance and wielding a whip, mercilessly tortures the sheep given to him by the first shepherd. This is the just "angel of punishment." The sheep are tangled in thorns and given no rest. The angel explains that the torture is temporal punishment for evil deeds, and once administered, the sheep are given to him for proper instruction and the sheep (i.e. men) learn to walk in the ways of the Lord with pure hearts. The punishment is not equal to the sin in duration, for torture imparts powerful memories. All acts that a man performs with pleasure are luxurious and invite punishment. Good works can satisfy a man and be to his benefit. Those who live in harmful luxury and do not repent are ultimately punished with death.

7. Hermas is told that he will be punished at the hands of the other shepherd for the sins of his family as he is the head of the household. Foreknowledge of the punishment is a blessing, as it is an assurance that the Lord finds Hermas worthy of proper instruction.

8. Hermas was shown the people of God standing under a willow tree. An angel gives him pruned branches from it. When summoned, they returned the branches to the angel in various states (about twelve) ranging from withered to green and fruitful. The people who brought back branches bearing fruit were crowned, and all who returned green branches were clothed in white and allowed to enter the tower. The remaining branches, all withered in some way, were planted by the shepherd to see if they grow (willows are very forgiving plants). After a few days, the planted branches were inspected and based on the results, some men were let into the tower while others were given dwellings in the walls around the tower, and yet others were lost altogether. The tree is revealed to be the "Law" that is the Son of God, and the angel to be Michael, who has been placed in charge of God's people. Those who could enter the tower were they who had suffered or been afflicted or at least maintained pure hearts.

9. Hermas, strengthened by the Holy Spirit, was visited by the angel of repentance so that he may be

instructed more perfectly. He was taken to Arcadia, to a hill on a plain surrounded by twelve mountains. The mountains varied in vegetation and appearance. In the plain was a large rectangular pillar, larger than the mountains and hewn from an old white rock with a gate guarded by twelve virgins. Many large men, led by six distinguished men, came to build a tower upon the stone. Ten shiny rectangular stones ascended from a pit and were taken through the gate and given to the men by the virgins to become the foundation of the tower. The three layers of stone that followed were built from an increasing number of stones, first twenty-five, then thirty-five, and then forty. Then colored stones were brought from the mountains and they became white when used to build the wall. Some stones were found unsuitable by the six leaders and were taken away and returned to their places of origin. The men rested after a time and the master for whom the tower was being built arrived to examine it. He tapped each stone thrice with a rod, revealing deformities and flaws in many. These were replaced by rectangular and circular stones found in a place where the master instructed them to look. The master instructed the Shepherd to clean the stones that had been replaced and to discard any that could not be cleaned. Assisted by the virgins and twelve other women dressed in black, the Shepherd amended all of the stones that he could, and they were added back into the tower.

When the tower was complete, the stones fit together seamlessly such that the tower appeared to have been hewn out of the rock at its base. The tower was then cleaned, and the grounds swept. As the Shepherd rested, Hermas stayed with the virgins, praying without ceasing and feasting on the words of the Lord.

The Shepherd then explained the vision to Hermas. The large white rock is the Son of God. He is old, for he existed before creation; through the gate in the rock is new, and through him, men (the stones) enter the kingdom of God. The master is also the Son of God, and the men building the tower—the Church—are his angels. The virgins are holy spirits, the powers of the Son of God. Four (named Faith, Continence, Power & Patience) are more powerful than the rest (Simplicity, Innocence, Purity, Cheerfulness, Truth, Understanding, Harmony, Love) Bearing the name of the Son of God is vital, but the stones must be carried into the tower by his powers. Conversely, the women in black are temptresses, and they carry away imperfect stones, though they who are not tempted and return to the ways of the virgins are added back to the tower. Four of these women (Unbelief, Incontinence, Disobedience & Deceit) are also more powerful than their followers (Sorrow, Wickedness, Wantonness, Anger, Falsehood, Folly, Backbiting

& Hatred). The four layers of stones were righteous men, prophets and ministers, and apostles and teachers of the Son of God who never left the company of the spirits and one another. The stones ascended from the pit because they were obliged to ascend through water, sealed with the name of the Son of God, and by the preaching of the Apostles and the teachers. The mountains are the twelve tribes living throughout the world which vary in understanding (color) until they were preached the Son of God and become alike in understanding (white). Some revert to their old ways and are then returned to their former places, some ultimately rejected, for the chastisement for wickedness is worse for those who know God than for those who have not known him. The tower (the Church) is purified when stones such as these are rejected. During the repair process, the Shepherd filled in the cracks on certain stones so that the stones' surfaces could be leveled. These stones are the men who had heard Shepherd's message and repented. The Shepherd concludes with a plea of repentance: "heal yourselves, therefore, while the tower is still building."

The messenger who had delivered Hermas to the Shepherd returned, knowledgeable of Hermas' progress, to confirm that he desired to stay under the protection of the Shepherd. Upon Hermas' confirmation, he is assigned several virgins to assist him in life but was warned that they would depart from his house should he do anything to defile it. Before departing, the angel urges Hermas to live in the commandments given to him and to make them known to others." [6]

Reception in the Early Church

Among early Christian second century texts, the SH seems to have enjoyed a remarkable authoritative reception in Late Antiquity.[7] The SH was highly esteemed in the early church, especially in Egypt among the Alexandrian Fathers; some of them saw it as part of the authorized books of the New Testament. However, suddenly and for unknown reasons, the SH was ignored. The Muratorian fragment rejects the canonicity of SH and excludes it from liturgical use but recommends it for private edification[8] on the grounds that it was written "very recently, in our own times."[9]

---

[6] Ibid.

[7] Dan Batovici, "The Shepherd of Hermas in Recent Scholarship on the Canon: A Review Article," *Annali Di Storia Dell'Esegesi* 34 (January 1, 2017): 89.

[8] Christian Tornau and Paolo Cecconi, eds., *The Shepherd of Hermas in Latin: Critical Edition of the Oldest Translation Vulgata* (Berlin: Walter de Gruyter & Co, 2014), 4.

[9] Muratorian Fragment, 74. See Michael J. Kruger, *Canon Revisited: Establishing the Origins and Authority of the New Testament Books* (Wheaton: Crossway, 2012), 281.

Origen calls it divinely inspired.[10] Tertullian although earlier in *De Oratione* 16 had respect for the SH, later he rejected it as dangerous,[11] he called it the "the Shepherd of Adulterers" (*Pud.* 10:12, 20:2). He viewed the piece as allowing for one-time repentance for adultery, which Tertullian opposed. Eusebius, in the fourth century, considers the SH a disputed, spurious book.[12] On the other hand, he testifies to the practice, even in his own days, of reading the SH publicly in some churches (*Ecc. Hist.* 3.3.6). In another reference, he says that Irenaeus describes the SH as "Scripture [γραφή]" (*Haer.* 4.20.2; *Ecc. Hist.* 5.8.7). Rufinus acknowledges that the SH was read in the church (*Comm. Symb.* 36). Athanasius, however, appointed the SH for catechetical instruction (*Ep. Fest.* 39).

Dating and Place of Origin

Some scholars, like Vielhauer, date it to AD 120-140 on internal grounds.[13] Goodspeed and Grant suggest that at least parts of the SH date to AD 95-100 because of

---

[10] (Origen, Commentarii in Romanos 16.14), cited in Peter Oakes, *Rome in the Bible and the Early Church* (Grand Rapids: Baker Academic, 2004), 158.

[11] Edmon L Gallagher and John D Meade, *The Biblical Canon Lists from Early Christianity: Texts and Analysis* (Oxford: Oxford University Press, 2017), 106 fn. 145.

[12] Gallagher and Meade, 103.

[13] John J Collins, *Apocalypse: The Morphology of a Genre*, Semeia 14 (Missoula: Society of Biblical Literature: distributed by Scholars Press, 1979), 74.

the reference to Clement of Rome in Vision 2; they propose that the work was composed in three stages and completed no later than AD 155[14] which is the traditionally accepted date.

According to Osiek and Koester, there can be little doubt that the geographical origin of The SH is central Italy and probably Rome."[15] Their scholarly agreement is based upon internal evidence such as references to Rome itself: the Tiber (Vis. 1.1-2), the Via Campana (Vis. 4.1.2), and the description of the vines grown on elm trees (Sim. 2).[16] Peterson offers another view of the place of origin. He argues that the Jewish aspect of the commandment and parables originates in a Palestinian ascetic milieu; all references to Rome are imaginary, and it is a methodological error to assume anything about Roman Christianity from the SH.[17] Other scholars do not find this view convincing.[18]

---

[14] Edgar Johnson Goodspeed and Robert McQueen Grant, *A History of Early Christian Literature* (Chicago: University of Chicago Press, 1983), 30–33; Cited in, Collins, *Apocalypse*, 74.

[15] Carolyn Osiek and Helmut Koester, *Shepherd of Hermas: A Commentary* (Minneapolis: Fortress Press, 1999), 18.

[16] Ibid., 18.

[17] See Erik Peterson, *Frühkirche Judentum und Gnosis: Studien und Untersuchungen* (Darmstadt: Wissenschaftliche Buchgesellschaft, 1982); in Osiek and Koester, *Shepherd of Hermas*, 1999, n. 136.

[18] Osiek and Koester, Ibid.

Authorship

Some scholars argue that this type of apocalyptic literature cannot be produced by ordinary people.[19] Ordinary people are here defined as lacking both the expertise and the resources to compose even a short epistle of the kind we find in early Christian literature. On the other hand, popular apocalyptic literature involves specialized expert authors who are meant to address ordinary people, whether in specific settings or for general consumption.[20] Especially considering Dibelius' suggestion that the SH is entirely allegorical,[21] we should assume an author with expertise.

While there is no indication that the SH is a pseudonym,[22] Baker summarizes the different opinions regarding the issue of authorship as follows:[23]

1) A single author, Hermas, wrote the work over an extended period from circa AD 90-120.

---

[19] John J Collins, *The Oxford Handbook of Apocalyptic Literature*, Oxford Handbooks (Oxford: Oxford University Press, 2014), 226.

[20] Collins, 226.

[21] Martin Dibelius, *Der Hirt des Hermas*, Apostolischen Väter 4 (Tübingen: J.C.B. Mohr, P. Siebeck, 1923).

[22] Collins, *Apocalypse*, 74.

[23] Ian Baker, "Shepherd of Hermas: A Socio-Rhetorical and Statistical-Linguistic Study of Authorship and Community Concerns" (PhD, Cardiff University, 2006), 2, http://orca.cf.ac.uk/56076/.

2) Three different authors wrote the SH. Author 1 wrote The Visions section between AD 100-140. Author 2 wrote Similitude *9* around the middle of the second century. Author 3 later added The Mandates and the remainder of The Similitudes. The whole text was completed circa AD 160.

3) Multiple authors wrote the SH. Up to seven different authors dating circa AD 70-130. This position is almost completely discarded. [24]

The Muratorian Fragment and the *Liber Pontificalis* (third century) identify the author as *frater* of Pope Pius I (AD 140-155).[25] Jerome, in the fourth century, has an interesting view on the SH:

> "Hermas whom the apostle Paul mentions in writing to the Romans *Salute Phlegon, Hermes, Patrobas, Hermas and the brethren that are with them* is reputed to be the author of the book which is called Pastor and which is also read publicly in some churches of Greece. It is, in fact, a useful book and many of the ancient writers quote from it as an

---

[24]For 'Multiple Authorship' theories see Carolyn Osiek and Helmut Koester, *Shepherd of Hermas: A Commentary* (Minneapolis: Fortress Pr, 1999), 8.
[25]Tornau and Cecconi, *The Shepherd of Hermas in Latin*, 1.

authority, but among the Latins, it is almost unknown." (*De Viris Illustribus* 10).[26]

So, it seems reasonable to follow the conclusion of Osiek, that the SH had a non-elite Greek-speaking context with limited literary education; this means that the SH "belonged" to the "common people" of the city.[27]

Literary Genre

Generally, the SH is considered an Apocalyptic genre. A few distinctive characteristics support that classification. Two important things must be taken into consideration: first, it is worth noting that the book does not call itself an apocalypse, in contrast to some other Jewish, Christian and Gnostic works that titled themselves apocalypse; second, we must differentiate between apocalypse as a literary genre, and apocalyptic eschatology as a religious perspective and structure of thought.[28] Collins gives a comprehensive definition of the genre that allows us to identify it with the SH:

> "Apocalypse is a genre of revelatory literature with a narrative framework, in which a revelation is mediated by an otherworldly being to a human recipient,

---

[26] "Church Fathers: De Viris Illustribus (Jerome)," accessed April 25, 2019, http://www.newadvent.org/fathers/2708.htm.
[27] Osiek and Koester, *Shepherd of Hermas*, 1999, 21.
[28] Collins, *Apocalypse*, 3.

disclosing a transcendent reality which is both temporal insofar as it envisages eschatological salvation and spatial insofar as it involves another, supernatural world."[29]

Still, different early Christian apocalypses follow very different literary paths and seem to serve diverse functions depending on their authors, social context, targeted audience, and function. [30]

Within the apocalyptic genre, the SH is categorized as a primary apocalyptic discourse, where it appeals to the speaker's direct reception of revelation.[31] Even though the SH fits the apocalyptic literary genre definition, some suggest that it cannot be considered as apocalyptic, or pseudo-apocalyptic as it lacks the visions of heaven that is central to other apocalypse literature and end-of-the-world catastrophic occurrences.[32] This suggestion is, however, based on a narrow definition of the apocalyptic genre.

The literary type of the SH leaves very little to say about its local church structure and its theological motifs, unlike the rest of the Apostolic Fathers corpus.[33] It is worth mentioning that the Muratorian Fragment groups it with the

---

[29] Collins, 9.

[30] Collins, *The Oxford Handbook of Apocalyptic Literature*, 232.

[31] Collins, 222.

[32] Baker, "Shepherd of Hermas," 1.

[33] Osiek and Koester, *Shepherd of Hermas*, 1999, 21.

Apocalypse of John and the *Apocalypse of Peter*. We might define the SH as an *Apocalyptic Discipline* since its aim is discipline and it addresses discipline issues.

Major Textual Witness

Various manuscripts containing fragments of the text have survived as follows: [34]

S	Codex Sinaiticus (4th cent.; contains 1.1–31.6)
A	Codex Athous (14th–15th cent.; contains 1.1–107.2)
Sc	later correctors of S
B	Bodmer Papyrus 38 (late 4th–early 5th cent.; contains 1.1–21.4)
M	Michigan Papyrus 129 (2nd cent.; contains 51.8–82.1)
L¹	the "Old Latin" or "Vulgate" translation (perhaps dating from the 2nd cent.). This is the text used for those portions of 107.3–114.5 for which no Greek text survives, and some of its manuscripts (A S

---

[34] Michael W. Holmes, *The Apostolic Fathers: Greek Texts and English Translations*, 3rd edition (Grand Rapids: Baker Academic, 2007), 448–49.

	Z) are occasionally cited individually.
L²	the "Palatine" Latin translation (usually dated to the 4th cent.)
L	L¹ + L²
E	the Ethiopic translation (perhaps 6th cent.)
F	fragments from a florilegium of patristic texts (Paris gr. 1143, 13th cent.): 52.8–10; 56.4–9; 66.4–5; 100.3–5; 110.1–3
P^{hamb}	Hamburg Papyrus 24 (53.6–54.5; 4th–5th cent.)
P^{am}	Amherst Papyrus II 190 (seven fragments, 5th–6th cent.)
Pber	Berlin Papyri (four fragments, 3rd–6th cent.)
Pm	Michigan Papyrus 130 (27.6–28.1; 2nd cent.)
Pox	Oxyrhynchus Papyri (twelve papyri, all from the 2nd/3rd to 4th cent.)
Ppr	Prague Papyrus 1 (three fragments; 4th–5th cent.)

Ant	Antiochus, Πανδέκτης τῆς ἁγίας γραφῆς (7th cent.)
Ath	Pseudo-Athanasius, Διδασκαλίαι πρὸς Ἀντίοχον; Ath1 and Ath2 indicate the readings of the two manuscripts of Pseudo- Athanasius where they differ
C1	Coptic translation, Akhmimic dialect (4th cent.)
C2	Coptic translation, Sahidic dialect (5th cent.)
C	C1+C2
Pers	Middle Persian translation (only fragments of which have been discovered)

Textual Transmission

The SH had a wide and interesting textual transmission history. As was shown above, its textual sources date from the third to the 14th century[35] in five different languages,[36] but the complete Greek text of the SH

---

[35] Tornau and Cecconi, *The Shepherd of Hermas in Latin*, 1.
[36] Tornau and Cecconi, 1.

does not survive in any single manuscript.[37] Actually, the Greek text was unknown in modern times until the discovery of *Codex Athous*[38] (A) in the 19th century which dates back to the fifteenth century and contains about 95 percent of the text.[39]

Structure

The SH cannot be considered as a text of a well-planned logical argument; rather it is known for its rambling content and style.[40] One of the unique features of the SH is its use of the church as a source of its revelations. This is atypical in the genre of apocalypses.[41] The SH seems logically divided into three parts: five visions, twelve mandates, and ten similitudes. However, the author himself divided it into two sections. The first section consists of the first four visions. The second section begins with the fifth vision and is followed by the mandates and similitudes

---

[37]L. W. Barnard, "The Shepherd of Hermas in Recent Study," *The Heythrop Journal* 9, no. 1 (January 1, 1968): 29, https://doi.org/10.1111/j.1468-2265.1968.tb00347.x.

[38]Osiek and Koester, *Shepherd of Hermas*, 1999, 1.

[39]A. Hilhorst, *Semitismes et latinismes dans le Pasteur d'Hermas* (Nijmegen: Dekker & Van de Vegt, 1976), 15.

[40] Baker, "Shepherd of Hermas," 224.

[41] Donald W. Riddle, "The Messages of the Shepherd of Hermas: A Study in Social Control," *The Journal of Religion* 7, no. 5/6 (October 1, 1927): 575–76.

Community and Function

The SH expresses a Jewish-Christian theological perspective by means of imagery, analogies, and parallels drawn from Roman society and culture, according to Holmes.[42] Velasco elaborates that the entire Jewish-Christian literature corpus is apocalyptic.[43]

Analyzing conflict language in the Greek text of the SH, Baker concludes:

> "Hermas *was* in conflict with the churches in Rome because of a changing attitude in the churches. Some Christians were more concerned about wealth and status than caring for others, and this criticism could be brought against the leaders too. He also appears to feel that personal holiness is lacking in the members of the churches beyond his own community. Hermas compares the present situation with the past, and how it used to be. Although his community seems to be a caring one and perhaps consisted of poorer members, it seems to be resisting the changes of the age

---

[42] Holmes, *The Apostolic Fathers*, 442.

[43] Jesús María Velasco, "Jewish Christianity of the First Centuries," *Biblical Theology Bulletin* 6, no. 1 (February 1, 1976): 9.

[...] It was already, at the time Hermas wrote, a community in crisis."[44]

Riddle shows that the SH,

"pictures a religious body in which the unity of the group is broken by differing attitudes, by a lack of unanimity which is exhibited [...] in matters of discipline."[45]

Wealth and richness caused problems in the church (Vis. 3.6.5, 6; Sim. 8.1.2; etc). This agrees with our definition of Hermas as an *Apocalyptic Discipline*.

Gregory suggests that the SH appears to take a different approach to the theology of post-baptismal sin from that portrayed in the Book of Hebrews, which suggests it exhibits theological creativity either independently of or in dialogue with Hebrews.[46] Some suggest that it appears to support a model of ministry that includes the charismatic alongside the institutional,[47] but this suggestion needs more investigation and is outside the scope of this work.

We can here conclude that the SH is a debatable document in every aspect: its authorship, canonicity, textual transmission, motif, and even its literary genre.

---

[44] Baker, "Shepherd of Hermas," 233–34.

[45] Riddle, "The Messages of *The Shepherd of Hermas*," 565.

[46] Oakes, *Rome in the Bible and the Early Church*, 149.

[47] Oakes, 150.

Chapter Two
Christology

The question of Christology is related to our understanding of the genre, community, audience, and the identification of the SH's purpose. We introduced these topics in the previous chapter, and we will use them to analyze the SH's Christology.

Another important issue must be taken into consideration before going further. The SH is not an epistle but an allegory or a religious romance.[48] This should impact our interpretation.

The most useful information on the SH's Christology and its view of the (Proto-)Trinity is found in Similitude (Sim.) 5 and Similitude 9. Some suggest that it is problematic to trace Similitude 5 to the overall author of the SH; many theories of multiple authorship have evolved, as mentioned in the previous section.[49] The best historical evidence based on an early use of the text indicates an initial

---

[48]Charles H. Hoole, *The Shepherd of Hermas* (Kessinger Publishing, LLC, 2010), vii.

[49]For Multiple Authorship theories, see Osiek and Koester, *Shepherd of Hermas*, 1999, 8.

unity of the SH that was later broken by the circulation of separate sections independently.[50]

Another important point in our investigation is the identification of authorship. Baker's conclusion is the most convincing. Based on a quantitative statistical-linguistic analysis technique, he reached the conclusion that Similitudes and Mandates had a common author, and that Similitude 5 does not display any different authorial characteristics to the rest of the SH.[51] He asserts that any structural relationship that may exist between this Similitude and the rest of the text is that of the single author's craft.[52]

The difficulties in the SH are not just confined to its textual problems. Some other important issues—suggested by several scholars—must be taken into consideration in our understanding of the Christology of the SH, namely the issue of Binitarianism[53] versus Trinitarianism, and Angelomorphic Christology and Pneumatology. In fact, the Christology and the Pneumatology of the SH are very debatable issues. Scholars hold a variety of views: for

---

[50] Osiek and Koester, 8.

[51] Baker, "Shepherd of Hermas," 158.

[52] Baker, 158.

[53] Here, the term "Binitarian" is used in contrast to "Trinitarian;" however, we may have used it in the rest of this chapter as a notion of the two figures, the Father and the Son but not in a contrast to the Trinitarian notion.

example, while Bucur concludes that the SH is aware of Trinitarian formulae;[54] Gieschen argues that the SH is more Binitarian than Trinitarian in its final form;[55] while Bacon says that the SH is not, in reality, Trinitarian at all.[56] Robert J. Hauck summarizes these debates by saying that Hermas may consist of "simple moralizing adoptionism, an imperfectly developed spirit-Christology, an angel-Christology, or the conflicting Christologies of several authors."[57] He also adds that Harnack asserted that the SH represented a straight Theodotian adoptionism.[58] Kelly noted the difficulty of fitting the SH's Christology into categories,

> "Hermas' theology was thus an amalgam of Binitarianism and adoptionism, though it made an attempt to conform to the triadic formula accepted in the Church."[59]

---

[54]Bogdan Gabriel Bucur, *Angelomorphic Pneumatology* (Leiden: Brill, 2009), 137.

[55]Charles A. Gieschen, *Angelomorphic Christology: Antecedents and Early Evidence* (Leiden: Brill, 1998), 128.

[56] Benjamin Wisner Bacon, "Two Forgotten Creeds," *Harvard Theological Review* 6, no. 03 (July 1913): 313, https://doi.org/10.1017/S0017816000013286.

[57]R. J. Hauck, "The Great Fast: Christology in the Shepherd of Hermas," *Anglican Theological Review* 75, no. 2 (1993): 187.

[58]Hauck, 187.

[59]J. N. D. Kelly, *Early Christian Doctrines: Revised Edition*, Revised edition (San Francisco: HarperOne, 1978), 94.

Grillmeier throws up his hands:

> "Here we get glimpses of the Christology and Trinitarian faith of the great church, but the confusion is great and cannot completely be put right [...The] SH lapses into the terminological equivocation of the early church [...] the SH can find no way out of this terminological confusion."[60]

Next, we will endeavor to resolve this dilemma through reviewing the possible interpretation of the SH's Christological and Pneumatological texts.

Monotheism

It is clear that the SH is monotheistic. A formula in Mandate 1.1 reads:

> "First of all, believe that God is one, who created all things and set them in order, and made out of what did not exist everything that is, and who contains all things but is himself alone uncontained."

Here, taking Jewish influence into consideration, the SH may be citing the *Shema*: God is the only creator of all

---

[60]Hauck, "The Great Fast: Christology in the Shepherd of Hermas," 188.

things and He sets everything in order, He created everything from nothing.

Jesus and Christ

The name Jesus never occurs in the SH, except once in a doubtful variant reading of Vis. 3.6.6. The title Christ appears only three times in very dubious manuscript variants (Vis. 2.2.8, 3.6.6, Sim. 9.18.1), though there is a number of references to "the Name," either of God or of the Son.[61] The omission of the personal name or title is puzzling[62] and may occur because of reverential avoidance.[63]

This absence of the title Christ extends too to the absence of any reference to the cross, crucifixion, or resurrection.[64] Wilson addressed this critical issue in his study of the five problems in the interpretation of the SH.[65]

---

[61]Osiek and Koester, *Shepherd of Hermas*, 1999, 34.

[62]Osiek and Koester, 34.

[63]Suggested by J. Christian Wilson (Five Problems in the Interpretation of *The Shepherd of Hermas*: Authorship, Genre, Canonicity, Apocalyptic, and the Absence of the Name "Jesus Christ" [Mellen Biblical Series 34; Lewiston/Queenston/Lampeter: Mellen, 1995] 73–79) on the basis of Jewish custom and the cosmic role of the Son in Sim. 9.14.5.

[64]Hauck, "The Great Fast: Christology in *The Shepherd of Hermas*," 187.

[65]See John Christian Wilson, *Five Problems in the Interpretation of the Shepherd of Hermas: Authorship, Genre, Canonicity, Apocalyptic, and*

The Name and the Son of God

The SH speaks in a definite way about the Son of God: the name of the Son of God is the only way to the kingdom, "for before people bear the name of the Son of God" (Sim. 9.16.3), "all the nations that dwell under heaven, when they heard and believed, were called by the name of the Son of God" (Sim. 9.17.4). The author also adds that "no one will enter the kingdom of God unless he receives the name of his Son" (Sim. 9.12.4), and "one cannot enter the kingdom of God except by the name of his Son" (Sim. 9.12.5). The Son of God is described as the "glorious man" (Sim. 9. 13.8), who is the only "entrance" (Sim. 9.12.6), there is no other way "than through his Son" (Sim. 9.12.6), even to the six "glorious angels" (Sim. 9.12.8) could not enter to "God's presence without him" (Sim. 9.12.8).

Other texts refer explicitly to the name of Son of God, who sustains all creation. This creates distance between the Son of God and all other creatures:

> "The name of the Son of God is great and incomprehensible and sustains the whole world. If, therefore, all creation is sustained by the Son of God, what do you think of those who are called by him and bear the

---

the Absence of the Name "Jesus Christ" (Lewiston: Edwin Mellen Press, 1996).

name of the Son of God and walk in his commandments" (Sim. 9.14.5).

This text may also indicate the authority of the Son of God as he is the one who gave commandments that should be obeyed.

Grillmeier rightly concludes that the name of the Son of God in the SH implies complete transcendence and preexistence[66] and it is clearly related to salvation (Vis. 4.2.4). We may rightly assume that these texts allude to Jesus Christ, especially as the redemptive significance[67] of Jesus' name is alluded to in several texts of the document in a more implicit way: it is related to the water which implicitly alludes to baptism through water (Sim. 9.16.2); the tower has been set on a foundation by the word of the almighty and glorious Name (Vis. 3.3.5). This is also supported by another text, saying baptized in the name of the Lord (Vis. 3.7.3). There are texts which deal with the suffering for the name: "for the sake of the name" (Vis. 3.1.9); "severe persecution, crosses, wild beasts, for the sake of the name" (Vis. 3.2.10); "suffers because of the

---

[66] Alois Grillmeier, *Christ in Christian Tradition: From the Apostolic Age to Chalcedon*, Second Edition, vol. I (Atlanta: John Knox Press, 1965), 42.

[67] Larry W. Hurtado, *Lord Jesus Christ: Devotion to Jesus in Earliest Christianity*, Pbk. Ed edition (Grand Rapids: W. B. Eerdmans Publishing Co., 2005), 602.

name" (Vis. 3.2.10); and, "suffered for the name of the Son of God" (Sim. 9.28.1).

Harris asserts that, Sim. 9 shows,

"high onomatology [i.e. the 'name' motif] by considering the Name as glorious, great and marvelous, incomprehensible, and finally the act of calling upon the Name."[68]

In Similitude 9, the Name is called glorious (ἔνδοξος) twice and in each of the two instances it is the Name of the Lord.[69] In Similitude 9, the Name shifts from attributed to the Father (Lord) to attributed to the Son. This expresses a high view of the Name, i.e. a high Christology. Harris also makes this conclusion as an assertion to the high view of the Name motif, as "Hermas understands the Name still to be the Name of the Father, now extended to the Son."[70]

The Christological motifs of the Name are very clear. In Similitude 8 and Similitude 9, the Name is "absolutely indispensable to salvation, and is borne by the believer," asserts Harris.[71] The Name,

---

[68] Michael D. Harris, "Christological Name Theology in Three Second Century Communities" (Doctoral Dissertation, Marquette University, 2013), 180, https://epublications.marquette.edu/dissertations_mu/270/.

[69] Harris, 180.

[70] Harris, 185.

[71] Harris, 195.

> "plays a role in the ecclesiological tower in both Vision 3 as well as Similitude 9. In Vision 3, the Name places the church upon its watery foundation. The shift to 'the Name of the Son of God' in Similitude 9 leads Hermas to alter the image so that the Name itself becomes the foundation upon which the church stands."[72]

As discussed earlier, the SH may be citing some form of *Shema* in Mandate 1.26. Taking into consideration this text with Similitude 9.14.5, they show that the commandments come from both Son of God and God, which may allude to the inclusion of Jesus into the authoritative *divine identity* of God. According to the SH, the

> "Lord has sworn by his Son that those who have denied their Lord have been rejected from their life, that is, those who now are about to deny him in the coming days."[73]

We may expect that Hermas is alluding to the Old Testament when God has sworn by himself. Yet Hermas replaced God with the Son, which may indicate that the Son belongs to the *divine identity*. We notice here both a High

---

[72] Harris, 196.

[73] Larry W. Hurtado, *Lord Jesus Christ: Devotion to Jesus in Earliest Christianity*, (Grand Rapids: Wm. B. Eerdmans Publishing Co., 2005), 465–467.

Christology and Pre-existent Christology,[74] "the Son of God is far older than all his creation, with the result that he was the Father's counselor in his creation" (Sim. 9.12.2). The Son of God is not identified here within the creation, but he is identified with the Father as an older counselor for his creation. We may also conclude that the SH's view of the Son of God can be seen based on four criteria which identify the God of Israel: covenant, sovereignty, preexistence, and creation, which confirms our conclusion of High Christology in the SH.

Svigel draws our attention to a possible High Christology case in Vision 2.2.8, where the Father is said to have *sworn by his own son* ("κατα τον υιον αυτου"). Svigel suggests that the author of the SH has had the principle in mind of God confirming vows *by himself* ("καθ εαυτου") since He could vow by no one greater (Hebrews 6:13).[75] He argues that since the author of 1 Clement knew the book of Hebrews, then it is quite plausible that Hermas—likewise writing from Rome in the same generation—also knew the book of Hebrews.[76] If this is right, then the SH is intentionally showing that the Son is as high as God the

---

[74] Hurtado, 603.

[75] Michael J. Svigel, "Trinitarianism In Didache, Barnabas, and the Shepherd: Sketchy, Scant, or Scandalous?," *Perichoresis* 17, no. 1 (March 1, 2019): 30.

[76] Svigel, 31.

Father, rendering a powerful allusion to a very high Christology.[77]

Angelomorphic and Angelic Christology

Before discussing the subject of Angelomorphic and Angelic Christology, the variety of Angelic figures in the SH must be mentioned. In his doctoral dissertation, Gieschen summarizes the following angelic figures in Hermas:[78]

The Angel of Repentance: who is identified as the Shepherd (Vis. 5.7), this angel appears several times and has no Christological motifs.

The Angel of Punishment: is referred to also as the Shepherd of Punishment in Similitude 6.2.5 with no Christological motifs.

The Most Revered Angel: is alluded to as the one who sent the Shepherd to Hermas in Vision 5.2 [...] Mandate 5.1.7 mentions that this angel justifies all the righteous.[79]

The Glorious Angel: directs the actions of the Angel of Punishment (Sim. 7.2-3). There is a link between the

---

[77] Svigel, 31.

[78] Charles A. Gieschen, "Angelomorphic Christology: Antecedents and Early Evidence" (Doctoral dissertation, University of Michigan, 1995), 238–42.

[79] Gieschen, 241.

Glorious Angel and the Angel of the Lord,[80] and is also identified as Michael in Similitude 7.3.3.

The Glorious Man: is identified as taller than the tower (Sim. 9.6.1) and as the Lord of the tower (Sim. 9. 7. 1). He is also identified as the Son of God in (Sim. 9.12.8) who has six angels supporting him.

The Angel of the Lord: is mentioned in Similitude 8.1.2: "he appears to be the same angel as the Glorious Angel and possibly also the Glorious Man."[81]

The Son of God: has the form of a servant (Sim. 5.2.1-11) and he appoints angels over people, cleanses people of their sins and gave them the law (Sim. 5.6.2-3). He is pre-existent and equated with the Spirit (Sim. 9.1.1) and is identified with the Name (Sim. 9.14.5-6).

Michael: The Glorious Angel is identified as Michael in Similitude 8.3.3.[82]

Definitions

A long debate over various definitions of the terms Angelomorphic and Angelic Christology ensues in the field today. Danièlou, Knight, Werner, Fletcher-Louis, Hannah

---

[80] Gieschen, 241.

[81] Gieschen, 242.

[82] Gieschen, 242.

and Hoffmann have all made defining contributions.[83] It is easy to define Angel Christology as a concept which regards Christ as an angel, or more broadly as an angelic being.[84] Angelomorphic, as described by Hoffmann, is "portraying a figure by relating it to the angelic world without implying that it actually represents an angel."[85] Therefore, Angelomorphic Christology is the identification of Christ with angelic form and functions[86] even though He may not be explicitly identified as an angel.[87]

Is the Son of God an Angel in the SH?

In his study, "Angelomorphic Christology: Antecedents and Early Evidence," Gieschen shows that Angelomorphic Christological traditions play a significant role in early Christology; he succeeds in confirming its relevance by showing that these traditions were used to assert that Christ is the visible manifestation of God.[88]

---

[83] Matthias Reinhard Hoffmann, "Angelomorphic Christology and the Book of Revelation" (Doctoral, Durham University, 2003), 22–25, http://etheses.dur.ac.uk/1740/.

[84] Hoffmann, 32.

[85] Hoffmann, 35.

[86] Hoffmann, 25.

[87] Gieschen, "Angelomorphic Christology: Antecedents and Early Evidence," 27–28; cited in Hoffmann, "Angelomorphic Christology and the Book of Revelation," 24.

[88] Gieschen, "Angelomorphic Christology: Antecedents and Early Evidence," 351.

In the SH, we come across a diversity of several Angelomorphic figures. Some signify Jewish influence while others are clearly Christological.[89] In one of the texts in the SH, Christ is called Michael, Velasco explains:

> "This is the development of the Jewish tradition according to which Michael received in charge the people of Israel, while the other angels were appointed for other people [...] For the church, he [Michael] is the Word of God who strips the angels of their functions and unites all nations under his scepter. In the *Pseudo-Clementine Homilies* (18:4) Michael, who gave the Law to Israel, is represented as reappearing in Christ."[90]

Velasco also points to a common feature of Jewish-Christian theology: giving a cosmic dimension to the events of the life of Christ, as Christ crosses the angelic world in His incarnation.[91]

According to Gieschen, there is "identification of Christ with angelic form and functions, either before or after the incarnation."[92] Jesus is described in the SH as "God's

---

[89] Gieschen, *Angelomorphic Christology*, 215.
[90] Velasco, "Jewish Christianity of the First Centuries," 21.
[91] Velasco, 22.
[92] Gieschen, *Angelomorphic Christology*, 27.

particular *angelos* (messenger)."[93] The Father sends Jesus as a special angel, called "most holy angel" (Vis. 5, 1.2), "glorious angel" (Sim. 9, 1.3) which according to Hurtado, is a role "associated exclusively with God in ancient Jewish tradition."[94]

The glorious angel in the SH functions like God (Yahweh): he judges souls, rewards the just, bestows grace, incorporates men into the church (Sim.8.1.1-2; 8.2.1-4).[95] It is seemingly nearer to an Old Testament understanding of *angel* [מלאך] than to any specific figure in later angelology. We can conclude that the glorious angel is equated with Yahweh.

Similitude 7.5 presents the figure of the "Angel of the Lord," who according to Similitude 8.1.2 is "glorious and very tall." In Similitude 9.6.1, a figure of the "Glorious Man" appears; he is taller than the tower. He is identified as Lord of the entire tower in Similitude 9.7.1. Later, Similitude 9.12.8 identifies him as the "Son of God." It appears clearly that the "Angel of the Lord" is the "Glorious Man'" who is the "Son of God" as in Similitude 8.3.3, where Michael, the great and *glorious* (ενδοξος) angel, is equated with the Son of God.

---

[93] Hurtado, *Lord Jesus Christ*, 2005, 604.

[94] Ibid., 605.

[95] Charles H Talbert, *The Development of Christology during the First Hundred Years: And Other Essays on Early Christian Theology* (Leiden: Brill, 2011), 100.

While this may be considered as primitive Angel Christology, Svigel argues that *glorious* (ενδοζος) is not used as a technical description of an individual angel, Michael, but as a general description of angels.[96] In the same way, he argues that the phrase "glorious man" is simply not a title or technical designation.[97] He ends his argument by stating,

> "therefore, equating the 'glorious angel' Michael and the 'glorious man' with the son of God is unwarranted. [...] In short, the SH never equates the Son of God with an 'angel.' We have consistent Christology in the SH in which the Son is distinct from the Father and the Spirit, though all three are divine and glorious."[98]

Son of God and the Holy Spirit: Similitude 9

The most controversial text regarding Christology and Pneumatology comes from Similitude 9: "...what the Holy Spirit that spoke with you in the form of the church revealed to you; for that spirit is the Son of God" (Sim. 9.1.1). It seems that for the SH the Son of God is the Holy Spirit, which may suggest that the author was Binitarian,

---

[96] Svigel, "Trinitarianism In Didache, Barnabas, and the Shepherd," 35.
[97] Svigel, 35.
[98] Svigel, 35.

not Trinitarian, or maybe he has yet another view we do not know about.

Bucur represents three of the most recent Christological interpretations of this puzzle. He states:

> Henne thinks of πνεῦμα as the trinitarian person of the Holy Spirit and rejects any ontological identification with the Son of God; he blames the confusion on a certain *'maladresse de l'expression'* in the text. For Brox, the puzzling relation between some of the major characters in the Shepherd can only be resolved by positing their identity. One would be well advised, however, not to read any theology into such statements, and instead only take note of the 'uncontrollable style' of the Shepherd. On the opposite end of the interpretative spectrum, Wilson is adamant that the author 'knew exactly what he was doing when he wrote Similitude 9.1.1,' and 'had a definite theological point to make,' albeit one whose explanation 'is left to the reader.' According to Wilson, this theological message was the following: God, who had a 'natural son,' the Holy Spirit, later transformed a high celestial entity into a second, 'adopted' son. This celestial entity was 'preexistent and served as counselor to God at the beginning of creation,' but it 'was

not at that time related to God as son to father (as was the Holy Spirit);' it became incarnate and after exemplary service in communion with the Spirit, was exalted to the status of 'adopted son.' The Christology of the Shepherd would consequently develop over the three stages of angelic pre-existence, incarnation and indwelling, and adoption.[99]

His solution is implied in the Jewish and Jewish-Christian practice of designating angelic beings by the term spirit.[100] In this practice, the Son of God is, technically, a "holy spirit," and all other "holy" spirits are subordinate to the Son of God, the supreme Holy Spirit.

The angel of repentance in Similitude 9.1.2 wanted to explain to Hermas the meaning of the parable. This explanation is done in the form of the church, which is the

---

[99] Philippe Henne, *La christologie chez Clément de Rome et dans le Pasteur d'Hermas* (Freibourg, Suisse: Editions universitaires, 1992), 225; Norbert Brox and Hermas, *Der Hirt des Hermas* (Göttingen: Vandenhoeck & Ruprecht, 1991), 531; John Christian Wilson, *Toward a Reassessment of the Shepherd of Hermas: Its Date and Its Pneumatology* (Lewinston: Mellen, 1993), 137; cited in B. G. Bucur, *Angelomorphic Pneumatology: Clement of Alexandria and Other Early Christian Witnesses* (Leiden: Brill, 2009), 122–23, https://doi.org/10.1163/ej.9789004174146.i-238.

[100] Bucur, *Angelomorphic Pneumatology: Clement of Alexandria and Other Early Christian Witnesses*, 123.

symbolic identity, the revealing agent,[101] and the revealer is the Son of God, who is alluded to by the Name, in "for the sake of the Name" (Vis. 3.1.9), and "crosses [...] for the sake of the Name" (Vision 3.2.10). To reconcile the designation of the Son of God as the "holy spirit," we must take in consideration that the revealing agent (i.e. Church) is described also as "angel" and "spirit"; this successive identification can be described safely under Levison's category *angelic spirit*.[102] The reader is to understand that the angelic spirit is not just any celestial entity: the angelic appearance conceals the Son, the Glory, and the Name.[103]

Moreover, according to Bucur, the most likely background of the identification of the old rock with the Son of God (Sim. 9.12.1–2) is Christological: 1 Corinthians 10:4 (Christ as the rock).[104] Similitude 9.1.1 does not posit two entities[105] but only one, the highest angelic spirit, the Son of God and not the polymorphic Holy Spirit.[106]

The Son of God is pre-existent in Similitude 9.12.2. It reads, "the Son of God is prior to existence than all of his creation, so that he would be the counselor over his creation

---

[101] Bucur, *Angelomorphic Pneumatology*, 120.

[102] Bucur, 120.

[103] Bucur, 120.

[104] Bucur, *Angelomorphic Pneumatology: Clement of Alexandria and Other Early Christian Witnesses*, 121.

[105] Bucur, 122.

[106] Bucur, 122.

with the Father." This statement indicates also a High Christology since the Son of God functions as an agent of creation or more preciously, a creator.

Similitude 5

Baker illustrates the structure of Similitude 5 as follows:

> "Similitude 5 seems to be a strange mixture of themes and ideas. It begins with questions related to fasting (Sim. 5.1); a parable about a vineyard follows (Sim. 5.2), which is a parable about 'true fasting.' This becomes apparent in Similitude 5.3 where the explanation of the parable is given. True fasting and care for the poor must go hand in hand. The difficulty arises in the fact that the parable itself mentions the vineyard owner's son. However, in the explanation of the parable in Similitude 5.3, the son is not mentioned. The son *is* mentioned in the allegorical interpretation in Similitude 5.4 and the remainder of the Similitude deals with the son-slave relation with respect to the Son of God. This raises the question as to whether a vineyard parable relating to fasting and a vineyard parable relating to the role of the son have been fused together in

this Similitude, either by Hermas or a later editor.[107]

The issue in Similitude 5.5.2, is that the passage "the son is the holy spirit, and the slave is the Son of God," is seen as restoration by most commentators.[108] The text becomes complicated in Similitude 5.6.1-3, where the son is the Son of God, not the Holy Spirit, it returns only to be the Holy Spirit in Similitude 5.6.5.[109] This ambiguity seems to result from awkward combining of different segments of interpretation and from later editing of different layers or editions of the text as the narrative developed and as the interpretations became more complex.[110]

This Similitude text presents two problems. The first problem found in Similitude 5.5.2 which is another text that designates the Son as "the Holy Spirit" (Sim. 5.5.2). The second problem is that the text implies Adoptionist Christology. Similitude 5.6.7 reads:

"In order that this flesh also, having served the spirit blamelessly, might have

---

[107] Baker, "Shepherd of Hermas," 13.

[108] This clause occurs only in the Vatican. It does not occur in Lips. (*Leipzig* manuscript), Pal. (*Palatine* manuscript), or in the Æth (*Æthiopic* version) Osiek and Koester, *Shepherd of Hermas*, 1999, 177.

[109] Osiek and Koester, 177.

[110] Osiek and Koester, 177. The identification of the Holy Spirit with the Son of God in Sim. 9.1.1 is deceptively different, for here, precisely the Holy Spirit is *not* the Son of God.

some place to live, and not appear to have lost the reward of its service. For all flesh in which the Holy Spirit has lived will if it proves to be undefiled and spotless, receive a reward."

Or possibly the SH has a pre-existent Christology, as evidenced in Similitude 5.6.5, that reads: "the preexistent holy spirit, which created the whole creation, God caused."

Stewart-Sykes warns that understanding this text is difficult because Similitude 5 is a parable followed by a series of explanations, rather than a simple theological statement.[111]

Spirit Christology in Similitude 5

Although Spirit Christology is a complex theological paradigm,[112] it can be defined as using the biblical symbol of God as Spirit—not the symbol Logos—to designate Christ. In other words, it refers to the use of spirit language to designate Christ. However, this proposed definition is self-consciously Trinitarian and clings confessionally to the ontological deity of Christ.[113]

---

[111] A Stewart-Sykes, "The Christology of Hermas and the Interpretation of the Fifth Similitude," *Augustinianum* 37 (January 1, 1997): 273.

[112] Kyle David Claunch, "The Son and the Spirit: The Promise and Peril of Spirit Christology," *SBJT* 19.1 (2015): 108.

[113] Claunch, 108.

The earlier solution proposed previously for Similitude 9, that Similitude 9.1.1 does not posit two entities but only one, the highest angelic spirit, the Son of God and not the polymorphic Holy Spirit should be taken into consideration. We should also note that the Son of God is described as "a slave but is presented in great power and lordship" (Sim. 5.6.1), and after that, he is designated with the title "holy spirit" (Sim. 5.6.2). The solution here appears in the coexistence of both a Servant Christology—similar to that of Philippians 2—and a Spirit Christology.[114] The context supports this view, as it talks about the authority of the Son of God, which was given by the Father in the creation (Sim. 5.6.1). The statement used by the SH is similar to what the Pauline statement about Christ in 2 Corinthians 3:17, "the Lord is the Spirit (ο δε κυριος το πνευμα εστιν)," where Paul seems to identify the Lord with the Spirit.[115]

One cannot ignore the Jewish influence on the SH's Parables and Mandates. For instance, Oskar Skarsaune and Reidar Hvalvik point to the fact that in the ethical sections of the SH, there are evident similarities to Jewish thought[116] as seen in the close parallel in the *Rule of Community* of

---

[114] Bucur, *Angelomorphic Pneumatology*, 127.

[115] P. J. A. M. Schoonenberg, "Spirit Christology and Logos Christology," *Bijdragen* 38, no. 4 (January 1, 1977): 351.

[116] Oskar Skarsaune and Reidar Hvalvik, *Jewish Believers in Jesus: The Early Centuries* (Grand Rapids, Michigan: Baker Academic, 2017), 213.

Qumran and Mandate 6.2.1-4. [117] Also, the angelology of the SH shows many points of contact with ancient Jewish literature.[118] Hvalvik argues that

> "there is no doubt about the affinities shared between the SH and ancient Jewish literature [...] The SH is a witness to the continuing influence of Jewish thought and notions on the Christian Community in Rome."[119]

Here, our most important influence is what Stewart-Sykes suggests, that:

> "the source of Hermas' parabolic narrative and theology is the same as that of the *meshalim* [rabbinic] [...] indeed the setting of this very parable [Sim. 5] in fact has been traced to a Jewish background."[120]

Taking in consideration both the suggestions of Spirit Christology and Jewish influence, one can say that this identification of the Spirit with Christ is related to the Jewish messianic tradition and Spiritual messianism as a Jewish aspect of Christian language.

---

[117] Skarsaune and Hvalvik, 213.

[118] Skarsaune and Hvalvik, 214.

[119] Skarsaune and Hvalvik, 213–14.

[120] Stewart-Sykes, "The Christology of Hermas and the Interpretation of the Fifth Similitude," 280.

The Son of God appears in the form of a servant in Similitude 5.2.1-11. However, Similiutde 5.6.2-3 explains that the Son of God appointed angels over people, cleansed people of their sins, and gave them the law. The Holy Spirit dwelt in Him according to Similitude 5.6.5-7. The previous text also asserts his pre-existence. He is identified with the Rock and the Door/Gate in Similitude 9.12.2. He is further identified with the Name in Similitude 9.14.5-6.[121] The holy spirit here is not the hypostasized Holy Spirit, it is simply the Son of God himself as a spirit. Here, the logic of Christology and the forthcoming Trinity are not jeopardized since the Holy Spirit—which is not the spirit meant in the text—is not identified as the pre-existent Christ.[122] The case seems to reappear almost unchanged in second-century expressions of spirit Christology.[123] In Justin Martyr's *First Apology*, we read a similar statement: "it is wrong, therefore, to understand the Spirit and the power of God as anything else than the Word"[124] (see also, Justin, *Dialogue with Trypho* 110.1; Irenaeus, *Against Heresies* 5.1.2 and

---

[121] Gieschen, *Angelomorphic Christology*, 217.

[122] Anthony Briggman, "Spirit-Christology in Irenaeus: A Closer Look," *Vigiliae Christianae* 66, no. 1 (2012): 3.

[123] Richard N. Longenecker, *Contours of Christology in the New Testament* (Grand Rapids, Mich: Wm. B. Eerdmans Publishing Co., 2005), 23.

[124] "Church Fathers: The First Apology (St. Justin Martyr)," accessed June 20, 2019, http://www.newadvent.org/fathers/0126.htm.

Proof of the Apostolic Teaching 71[125]). Schoonenberg argues that traces of such Spirit Christology are preserved in the Syrian church and some isolated authors such as Lactantius where the word "spirit" is used to design Christ's divinity.[126] We may say that the SH use of the word *holy* (αγιον) before the word *spirit* (πνευμα) is done for the sake of veneration and exaltation.

Note, that the author mentioned the "great labor and enduring much toil" (Sim. 5. 6.2) which is done by the Son in order to "cleanse the sins of the people" (Sim. 5. 6.3). We may also assume—however hypothetically—that "the paths of life" (Sim. 5. 6.3) is the labor which is similar to the work of Christ reflected in Philippians 2. Now, we may conclude with Hurtado that,

> "the SH simply echoes traditional beliefs about Jesus as the unique agent of divine redemption, who undergoes sufferings in fulfillment of his obedience to the Father, as a consequence of which he is now the authoritative 'Lord' through whose teaching the redeemed are now required to exhibit their obedience to God."[127]

---

[125] Briggman, "Spirit-Christology in Irenaeus," 14.

[126] Schoonenberg, "Spirit Christology and Logos Christology," 354.

[127] Hurtado, *Lord Jesus Christ*, 2005, 603.

This matches a Spirit Christology, where it thematizes Christian experience of Jesus and explains the meaning of Jesus' being the bringer of God's salvation.[128] Haight adds,

> "in a Spirit Christology it becomes plain that the salvation mediated by Jesus is closely bound up with the way one lives in the Spirit; this salvation thus has a bearing on our lives in history." [129]

Non-Christological Reading of Similitude 5

The second problem is whether the Christology in Similitude 5 is Adoptionist or pre-existent. This matter is resolved when the text is read in the right, non-Christological way as suggested by Bucur.[130] Similitude 5 is a parable about true fasting and purity. This is how it was understood by Hermas (Sim. 5.1.1-5) and this is how the Shepherd introduced it: "Listen to the parable ($\pi\alpha\rho\alpha\beta o\lambda\eta\nu$) that I am about to tell you about fasting" (Sim. 5.2.1). It is suggested that this Similitude must be understood in its narrative as a parable about fasting and not from a Christological perspective. Stewart-Sykes explains what a parable is:

---

[128] Roger Haight, "The Case for Spirit Christology," *Theological Studies* 53, no. 2 (June 1, 1992): 286.

[129] Haight, 286.

[130] Bucur, *Angelomorphic Pneumatology*, 128, 131.

"A parable may be defined as 'indirect discourse.' Part of its indirectness consists in its narrative form; a narrative is always oblique, and so a parable is a deliberately oblique communication, it is intentionally ambiguous, and susceptible of multiple allusions and interpretations. When Hermas seeks a solution to the *parable* (παραβολη) he is recognizing the obliqueness of this mode of communication. But the solution is not simply a solution, it is itself a particular mode of indirect communication because in the narrative context of Hermas the application of the parable is a continuation of the overall narrative."[131]

Then Similitude 5, which is about fasting, should not be read Christologically but rather it should be read as anthropological and soteriological,[132] where the servant of God attains adoption by God through good works. And since Christ shows the perfection of humanity in the obedience of his flesh to the divine spirit within him, obedience which provides a model for imitation,[133] the

---

[131] Stewart-Sykes, "The Christology of Hermas and the Interpretation of the Fifth Similitude," 276.

[132] Stewart-Sykes, 275.

[133] Stewart-Sykes, 279.

Spirit of God may likewise dwell in human flesh just as it dwelt in the flesh of the Son of God.

We can say that the spirit which lives in flesh refers to all Christian believers,[134] taking in consideration the immediate context when the angel said to Hermas: "keep this flesh of yours clean and undefiled" (Sim. 5. 7.1). So, we may rightly assume that this parable is concerned with giving believers an incentive to live virtuous lives.[135] Here, the Shepherd concludes with a general ethical application of the parable.[136] We can say that Hermas is concerned to unite the themes of morality and Christology, by uniting the status and works of the servant of God with those of the Son of God.[137] Hauck points out, that here we are in front of an ethically motivated Christology, "since Christ shows the perfection of humanity in the obedience of his flesh to the divine spirit within him, an obedience which provides a model for imitation."[138]

To thread all the previous pieces of evidence, we can agree with Hurtado's conclusion that the SH is not

---

[134] Bucur, *Angelomorphic Pneumatology*, 131.

[135] Hurtado, *Lord Jesus Christ*, 2005, 603.

[136] Stewart-Sykes, "The Christology of Hermas and the Interpretation of the Fifth Similitude," 275.

[137] Stewart-Sykes, 279.

[138] Stewart-Sykes, 279; See: Robert John Hauck, "The Great Fast: Christology in the Shepherd of Hermas," *Anglican Theological Review* 75, no. 2 (1993): 187–98.

espousing an *adoptionist* Christology.[139] Henne argues that Christological results should not be squeezed out of an ethical parable that is initially about fasting; he also argues that,

> "the Christological reinterpretation of the parable stops at Similitude 5.6.4a, and that the subsequent verses are not Christological but rather concerned with the ascetic reshaping of the believer."[140]

For example, for Henne, the verse "flesh in which the Holy Spirit dwelled" would not be the man Jesus, but rather the Christian believer.[141] The SH then is not a Christological elaboration but embodies a High Christology as the starting point to elaborate ethical and ascetic issues. Sykes states that the Jewish origin of this ethical Christology can be linked with the Qumran community role in the salvific effect of the victory within the man of the Spirit of God.[142]

---

[139] Hurtado, *Lord Jesus Christ*, 2005, 603.

[140] Henne, *La christologie chez Clément de Rome et dans le Pasteur d'Hermas*; in Bucur, *Angelomorphic Pneumatology: Clement of Alexandria and Other Early Christian Witnesses*, 127–28.

[141] Henne, *La christologie chez Clément de Rome et dans le Pasteur d'Hermas*; in Bucur, *Angelomorphic Pneumatology: Clement of Alexandria and Other Early Christian Witnesses*, 131.

[142] Graydon F. Snyder, *The Apostolic Fathers: A New Translation and Commentary, Vol. VI, The Shepherd of Hermas* (Thomas Nelson and

In general, according to Hauck, the most serious sin in Hermas' message is 'double-mindedness,' the dangerous condition of *dipsychia*.[143] The *SH* main theme is repentance [μετάνοια]—or as translated by Aldo Tagliabue—"inner change"[144] and purity. It is not a Christological or Theological treatise.[145]

On the Use of "Spirit"

The final point we must take into consideration - the exact meaning of the "holy spirit" in the text must be understood carefully. The author described previously that the Holy Spirit as a real identity speaking in the "form" of church,[146] [i.e. the Church], which is a symbolic identity. Given the request made by Hermas from the "Lord to reveal to me the revelation" (Vision 3.1.2) and taking in consideration the Lord's reply "through the mouth of the elderly woman" (Vision 3, 1.2); it appears that the same is here also, the holy spirit can be viewed symbolically not as a real identity.

Sons Ltd., 1968), 108; in Stewart-Sykes, "The Christology of Hermas and the Interpretation of the Fifth Similitude," 284.

[143] Hauck, "The Great Fast," 189.

[144] Aldo Tagliabue, "Learning from Allegorical Images in the Book of Visions of the Shepherd of Hermas," *Arethusa*, no. 50 (2017): 221.

[145] Hauck, "The Great Fast," 188.

[146] Bucur, *Angelomorphic Pneumatology*, 120.

The SH's intended meaning of the words spirit (πνεῦμα) and spirits (πνεύματα) is not always apparent,[147] and deciding what the words exactly reference is sometimes difficult or impossible.[148] Bucur argues that the SH in many cases uses πνεῦμα for angelic entities and at other times for the Son of God.[149] He concludes that the SH uses spirit (πνεῦμα) as in the Jewish apocalyptic framework to refer to an angelic presence or more.[150] The SH also uses spirit language in Mandates 11 where he talks about the prophet, according to Bucur. The SH in Mandate 11.9 uses angel for the very same reality that it had described as an indwelling spirit.[151] Here, a distinction between real and symbolic identity must be drawn, Bucur gives the example of Similitude 9.1.1 where we see the real identity *the holy spirit* (τὸ πνεῦμα τὸ ἅγιον), and the symbolic identity, *the form is that of the church* (ἐν μορφῇ τῆς ἐκκλησίας).[152]

---

[147] Arden Conrad Autry, "Christ and the Spirit in the New Testament and in Christian Thought of the Second Century: A Comparative Study in Pneumatology" (Doctoral Dissertation, Baylor University, 1983), 218.

[148] Autry, 219.

[149] Bucur, *Angelomorphic Pneumatology: Clement of Alexandria and Other Early Christian Witnesses*, 114.

[150] Bucur, 116.

[151] Bucur, 117.

[152] Bucur, 120.

Conclusion

The SH mentions the three persons of the Trinity respectively: "for the Lord has tested you and has enrolled you among our number, and all your descendants will live with the Son of God, for you have partaken of his spirit" (Sim. 9.24.4).

This text reflects a primitive understanding of the Trinity reflected in an ethical way (testing/live with/partaken).

The SH is apparently a vague text in many parts like many other visionary texts, and some texts will remain problematic to later Christian Trinitarian articulations. However, it uses a primitive awareness of Trinitarian language. Bodgan concluded that:

> "Since the terms Father, Son, and Holy Spirit occur in Hermas Similitude 5, as part of a theological reinterpretation of the initial parable, there can be no doubt that the Shepherd was aware of Trinitarian formulas."[153]

Though we may not find this approach to the Trinity in either proto/later-orthodox or in the proto/later-heterodox

---

[153] Bucur, *Angelomorphic Pneumatology*, 137.

texts, its significance is that there is a Trinitarian understating found in an early unique type of literature.

Several interpretations have been suggested for Similitude 5 and Similitude 9 which presents the major parts of a probable Christological significance. Svigel asserts that,

> "we must remember that Similitude 5 is not an excursus on Christology and pneumatology, but a homily on Christ's example for all Spirit-indwelled Christians."[154]

He adds,

> "as perplexing as it may be for modern minds, we must not lose sight of the fact that we are dealing with the fluid vocabulary and syntax of visions and parables, not with the fixed logic of scholarly treatises."[155]

Angelic, Angelomorphic and Spirit Christology may also be found in the SH, with, undoubtedly, strong indication of a High Christology. One might agree with Svigel that the SH may be puzzling, peculiar, and perplexing, but it does not present an insurmountable

---

[154] Svigel, "Trinitarianism In Didache, Barnabas, and the Shepherd," 33.
[155] Svigel, 34.

problem for nascent trinitarianism, and it can easily be read in conformity

> "with a classic incarnational narrative of the divine Son distinct from the Spirit, both sent by the Father to accomplish the divine plan of creation, revelation, and redemption."[156]

Martin Dibelius proposes that many of the inconsistencies resulted from the underlying Jewish tradition of the SH not being fully Christianized by the author.[157,158] Lampe proposes several types of literature that Hermas relied on like Vergil's Bucolica, where timidly the SH reveals that his literary figures are dependent upon pagan prototypes.[159] Also, Stoic, popular pagan materials, and Hellenistic-Jewish traditions can be easily encountered in Hermas.[160] Another notion that supports Dibelius, Hermas knows only the law of God (Sim. 8.3.2) but no law of Christ; the whole Gospel for him is Baptism and Law.[161]

---

[156] Svigel, 35.

[157] See Martin Dibelius, *Der Hirt Des Hermas*, n.d.

[158] Gieschen, *Angelomorphic Christology*, 220.

[159] Peter Lampe, *From Paul to Valentinus: Christians at Rome in the First Two Centuries*, 1st Fortress Press Ed edition (Minneapolis: Augsburg Fortress Publishers, 2003), 228.

[160] Lampe, 230.

[161] Wilhelm Pratscher, ed., *The Apostolic Fathers: An Introduction* (Waco, Tex: Baylor University Press, 2010), 229.

Nobert Brox states[162] that the SH's Christology developed in a very fragmentary manner and is, therefore, difficult to systematize,[163] and even difficult to present as Christological motif of first or early second century. This also can be accounted to the several supposed authors who participated in the textual formation of the SH. The absence of the terms Jesus and Christian and the absence of direct quotations of both the Old and the New Testament or even alluding to them may also support Dibelius idea. But there are much to be taken into consideration before accepting Dibelius ideas and the multiple authors' hypothesis.

One of the most important question concerning Hermas is why it was never considered Christological heresy. On the contrary, it was regarded as Scripture by Irenaeus, Clement of Alexandria and Tertullian.[164] Kelly suggested that the SH's Christology was a mixture of Binitarianism and Adoptionism, though it made an attempt to conform to the triadic formula accepted in the Church.[165] Despite the enigma and puzzling issues of the SH, the more puzzling, however, is the fact that this text never

---

[162]See *Der Hirt Des Hermas* (Göttingen: Vandenhoeck & Ruprecht, 1991).

[163]Gieschen, *Angelomorphic Christology*, 220.

[164]F. L. Cross and E. A. Livingstone, eds., *Dictionary of the Christian Church*, 3rd edition (Peabody, Mass.; Edinburgh: Hendrickson Publishers, 2007), 760.

[165]Kelly, *Early Christian Doctrines*, 94.

scandalized its contemporaries or later orthodoxy[166] and was never condemned for heresy. That means it was viewed as a text that involves orthodox Christological/Trinitarian notions.

Taking the history of its transmission and the textual problems in consideration, plus a lack of systematic unity in the SH's Christology—a spirit/wisdom/nomos/angel Christology can all be found—suggests that there are different sources behind the work and, perhaps different authors[167] in different periods of time.

---

[166] Bucur, *Angelomorphic Pneumatology: Clement of Alexandria and Other Early Christian Witnesses*, 114.

[167] Barnard, "The Shepherd of Hermas in Recent Study," 33.

Bibliography

Autry, Arden Conrad. "Christ and the Spirit in the New Testament and in Christian Thought of the Second Century: A Comparative Study in Pneumatology." Doctoral Dissertation, Baylor University, 1983.

Bacon, Benjamin Wisner. "Two Forgotten Creeds." *Harvard Theological Review* 6, no. 03 (July 1913): 294–315. https://doi.org/10.1017/S0017816000013286.

Baker, Ian. "Shepherd of Hermas: A Socio-Rhetorical and Statistical-Linguistic Study of Authorship and Community Concerns." Doctoral Dissertation, Cardiff University, 2006. http://orca.cf.ac.uk/56076/.

Barnard, L. W. "The Shepherd of Hermas in Recent Study." *The Heythrop Journal* 9, no. 1 (January 1, 1968): 029–036. https://doi.org/10.1111/j.14682265.1968.tb00347.x.

Batovici, Dan. "The Shepherd of Hermas in Recent Scholarship on the Canon: A Review Article." *Annali Di Storia Dell'Esegesi* 34 (January 1, 2017): 89–105.

Briggman, Anthony. "Spirit-Christology in Irenaeus: A Closer Look." *Vigiliae Christianae* 66, no. 1 (2012): 1–19.

Brox, Norbert, and Hermas. *Der Hirt des Hermas.* Göttingen: Vandenhoeck & Ruprecht, 1991.

Bucur, B. G. *Angelomorphic Pneumatology: Clement of Alexandria and Other Early Christian Witnesses.* Leiden: Brill, 2009. https://doi.org/10.1163/ej.9789004174146.i-238.

Bucur, Bogdan Gabriel. *Angelomorphic Pneumatology.* Leiden: Brill, 2009.

"Church Fathers: De Viris Illustribus (Jerome)." Accessed April 25, 2019. http://www.newadvent.org/fathers/2708.htm.

"Church Fathers: The First Apology (St. Justin Martyr)." Accessed June 20, 2019. http://www.newadvent.org/fathers/0126.htm.

Claunch, Kyle David. "The Son and the Spirit: The Promise and Peril of Spirit Christology." *SBJT* 19.1 (2015): 91–112.

Collins, Billie Jean. *The SBL Handbook of Style: For Biblical Studies and Related Disciplines.* Atlanta: SBL Press, 2014.

Collins, John J. *Apocalypse: The Morphology of a Genre.* Semeia 14. Missoula: Society of Biblical Literature: distributed by Scholars Press, 1979.

———. *The Oxford Handbook of Apocalyptic Literature.* Oxford: Oxford University Press, 2014.

Cross, F. L., and E. A. Livingstone, eds. *Dictionary of the Christian Church.* Peabody: Hendrickson Publishers, 2007.

Der Hirt Des Hermas. Göttingen: Vandenhoeck & Ruprecht, 1991.

Dibelius, Martin. *Der Hirt des Hermas.* Apostolischen Väter 4. Tübingen: J.C.B. Mohr, P. Siebeck, 1923.

———. *Der Hirt Des Hermas*, n.d.

Foster, Paul. *The Writings of the Apostolic Fathers.* Bloomsbury Publishing, 2007.

Gallagher, Edmon L, and John D Meade. *The Biblical Canon Lists from Early Christianity: Texts and Analysis.* Oxford: Oxford University Press, 2017.

Gieschen, Charles A. "Angelomorphic Christology: Antecedents and Early Evidence." Doctoral, Michigan, 1995.

———. *Angelomorphic Christology: Antecedents and Early Evidence.* Leiden: Brill, 1998.

Goodspeed, Edgar Johnson, and Robert McQueen Grant. *A History of Early Christian Literature.* Chicago: The University of Chicago Press, 1983.

Grillmeier, Alois. *Christ in Christian Tradition: From the Apostolic Age to Chalcedon.* Second

Edition. Vol. I. Atlanta: John Knox Press, 1965.

Haight, Roger. "The Case for Spirit Christology." *Theological Studies* 53, no. 2 (June 1, 1992): 257–87.

Harris, Michael D. "Christological Name Theology in Three Second Century Communities." Doctoral dissertation, Marquette University, 2013. https://epublications.marquette.edu/dissertations_mu/270/.

Hauck, R. J. "The Great Fast: Christology in the Shepherd of Hermas." *Anglican Theological Review* 75, no. 2 (1993): 187–98.

Hauck, Robert John. "The Great Fast: Christology in the Shepherd of Hermas." *Anglican Theological Review* 75, no. 2 (1993): 187–98.

Henne, Philippe. *La christologie chez Clément de Rome et dans le Pasteur d'Hermas*. Freibourg: Editions universitaires, 1992.

Hilhorst, A. *Semitismes et latinismes dans le Pasteur d'Hermas*. Nijmegen: Dekker & Van de Vegt, 1976.

Hoffmann, Matthias Reinhard. "Angelomorphic Christology and the Book of Revelation." Doctoral dissertation, Durham University, 2003. http://etheses.dur.ac.uk/1740/.

Holmes, Michael W. *The Apostolic Fathers: Greek Texts and English Translations.* Grand Rapids: Baker Academic, 2007.

Hoole, Charles H. *The Shepherd Of Hermas.* Kessinger Publishing, LLC, 2010.

Hurtado, Larry W. *Lord Jesus Christ: Devotion to Jesus in Earliest Christianity.* Grand Rapids: W. B. Eerdmans Publishing Co., 2005.

———. *Lord Jesus Christ: Devotion to Jesus in Earliest Christianity.* Grand Rapids: W. B. Eerdmans Publishing Co., 2005.

Kelly, J. N. D. *Early Christian Doctrines:* San Francisco: HarperOne, 1978.

Kruger, Michael J. *Canon Revisited: Establishing the Origins and Authority of the New Testament Books.* Wheaton: Crossway, 2012.

Lampe, Peter. *From Paul to Valentinus: Christians at Rome in the First Two Centuries.* Minneapolis: Augsburg Fortress Publishers, 2003.

Longenecker, Richard N. *Contours of Christology in the New Testament.* Grand Rapids: W. B. Eerdmans Publishing Co., 2005.

Oakes, Peter. *Rome in the Bible and the Early Church.* Grand Rapids: Baker Academic, 2004.

Osiek, Carolyn, and Helmut Koester. *Shepherd of Hermas: A Commentary.* Minneapolis: Fortress Press, 1999.

———. *Shepherd of Hermas: A Commentary.* Minneapolis: Fortress Press, 1999.

Peterson, Erik. *Frühkirche Judentum und Gnosis: Studien und Untersuchungen.* Darmstadt: Wissenschaftliche Buchgesellschaft, 1982.

Pratscher, Wilhelm, ed. *The Apostolic Fathers: An Introduction.* Waco: Baylor University Press, 2010.

Riddle, Donald W. "The Messages of the Shepherd of Hermas: A Study in Social Control." *The Journal of Religion* 7, no. 5/6 (October 1, 1927): 561–77.

Schoonenberg, P. J. A. M. "Spirit Christology and Logos Christology." *Bijdragen* 38, no. 4 (January 1, 1977): 350–75.

"Shepherd of Hermas Explained | Brandon's Notepad." Accessed June 15, 2019. https://brandonsnotepad.wordpress.com/tag/shepherd-of-hermas-explained/.

Skarsaune, Oskar, and Reidar Hvalvik. *Jewish Believers in Jesus: The Early Centuries.* Grand Rapids: Baker Academic, 2017.

Snyder, Graydon F. *The Apostolic Fathers: A New Translation and Commentary, Vol. VI, The*

Shepherd of Hermas. Thomas Nelson and Sons Ltd., 1968.

Stewart-Sykes, A. "The Christology of Hermas and the Interpretation of the Fifth Similitude." *Augustinianum* 37 (January 1, 1997): 273–84.

Svigel, Michael J. "Trinitarianism In Didache, Barnabas, and the Shepherd: Sketchy, Scant, or Scandalous?" *Perichoresis* 17, no. 1 (March 1, 2019): 23–40.

Tagliabue, Aldo. "Learning from Allegorical Images in the Book of Visions of the Shepherd of Hermas." *Arethusa*, no. 50 (2017): 221–55.

Talbert, Charles H. *The Development of Christology during the First Hundred Years: And Other Essays on Early Christian Theology.* Leiden: Brill, 2011.

Tornau, Christian, and Paolo Cecconi, eds. *The Shepherd of Hermas in Latin: Critical Edition of the Oldest Translation Vulgata.* Berlin: Walter de Gruyter & Co, 2014.

Velasco, Jesús María. "Jewish Christianity of the First Centuries." *Biblical Theology Bulletin* 6, no. 1 (February 1, 1976): 5–26.

Wilson, John Christian. *Five Problems in the Interpretation of the Shepherd of Hermas: Authorship, Genre, Canonicity, Apocalyptic, and the Absence of the Name "Jesus Christ."* Lewiston: Edwin Mellen Press, 1996.

———. *Toward a Reassessment of the Shepherd of Hermas: Its Date and Its Pneumatology.* Lewinston: Mellen, 1993.

About the Author

Mina Fouad Tawfike is a Lecturer on the History of Christianity in Egypt and Tunisia at the Alexandria School of Theology. Mina holds both a BSc in Accounting, and a BTH, MA and MTh in Theology. Among his published works are: *The Coptic Church and its Political Challenges* with Beshoy Ramzy; *In the Image of God: The Worldwide Church and its Political Mission; Abū Rā'iṭa al-Takrītī: A Case Study for the Renewal of the Coptic Orthodox Doctrine of the Oneness of God*, with Emad Atef, published in ASJ Volume 2,; *Iskindiriyya Kaman W Kaman: Alessandria, La Rivoluzione E Il Desiderio Di Risorgere*, Limes: Rivista Italiana Di Geopolitica, Volume 21299, with Mena Milad.

He also contributed to photography. He published photographs of Egypt in *Historical Atlas of Ancient Christianity*, published by ICCS Press.

www.ingramcontent.com/pod-product-compliance
Lightning Source LLC
Chambersburg PA
CBHW030532080526
44586CB00011B/404